BUTTERFLIES

ann Chontae

AND

MOTHS

This edition 2003

Franklin Watts
96 Leonard Street
LONDON
EC2A 4XD

Franklin Watts Australia
45–51 Huntley Street
Alexandria
NSW 2015

Copyright © 1991 Franklin Watts

ISBN 0 7496 5004 4

Esitor: Hazel Poole
Design: K and Co
Consultant: Michael Chinery

Printed in Italy

KEEPING MINIBEASTS

Butterflies and Moths

Text and Photographs: Barrie Watts

CONTENTS

W

FRANKLIN WATTS
LONDON • SYDNEY

Moths and butterflies are colourful insects that can be found all over the world. Their bodies are very similar, but there are certain differences. Moths are normally active at night and butterflies fly during the day.

Another difference is the shape of their antennae. A butterfly's antennae are thicker at the end, like a club, but a moth's are normally thin and threadlike, sometimes like a feather.

Moths and butterflies live in many different sorts of habitats. This can be anywhere in the world, from a desert to a mountain. During the spring and summer, moths and butterflies can be found in most places in the countryside, especially near flowers. Butterflies, in particular, like to drink flower nectar, sucking in the liquid with their long, hollow tongues.

Collecting butterflies

The best way to look at butterflies is close up. However, this is difficult to do because they are shy and will fly away if you get too close to them. A large butterfly net will enable you to catch them without damaging them.

Take care not to touch them with your fingers
because they have fragile bodies and wings.
Use small cardboard tubs and boxes with
airholes to take them home in.

Collecting moths

Moths are often more difficult to catch as they are active at night. The easiest way to catch moths is to search for them resting on trees and fences in the daytime, but they are also

attracted to bright lights at night. You can even make your own moth light to put in the garden by using a lightbulb on a stick. If you put a white sheet underneath it, the moths will drop down from the light and be easier to see. You will need to ask a grown-up to set this up for you.

Housing

Butterflies and moths must be kept in large cages if you intend to keep them at home. The best type of cage is a round net cylinder at least one metre wide.

This can be hung up indoors or outside, or even made to stand up by itself by putting thin pieces of wood inside. Butterflies are more active when they are warm, so keep the cage by a sunny window.

If you want to make your own net cage, all you need is a big cardboard box, some fine netting, scissors and sticky tape. Cut a large window out

of the four sides leaving the top and bottom as they are, and fix the netting to the windows. This type of cage must be used indoors otherwise it will collapse if it gets wet.

All butterflies and
some moths will need
to be fed if you are
keeping them in cages.
The easiest way to do
this is to put some
fresh flowers in a jar of
water and place it in
the cage.

The flower nectar will give the insects all the food they need. Another way is to make a honey and water solution. Mix nine parts of water to one of honey and then soak some cotton wool with it. Place this in the cage and replace it when it gets dry.

Breeding

If you have a male and female moth or butterfly, it is best to put some of the correct caterpillar foodplant into the cage. A female butterfly lays her eggs only on the type of plant the young need as food, so find out what type of plant you will need. Keep it fresh by placing it in jars of water.

21

Life-cycle

The eggs hatch into caterpillars that feed and change their skins several times before becoming pupae (chrysalis). Some caterpillars burrow into the ground before turning into pupae, but butterfly pupae are usually attached to plant stems. This swallowtail pupa is attached to a fennel stalk.

Just before the butterfly is ready to emerge, the pupa changes colour. The swallowtail butterfly breaks out of the pupal case by pressing from inside until it splits.

A butterfly emerges

The swallowtail struggles out of the pupa and rests on it while blood flows into its wings. At this stage the wings are soft and crumpled and the butterfly cannot fly.

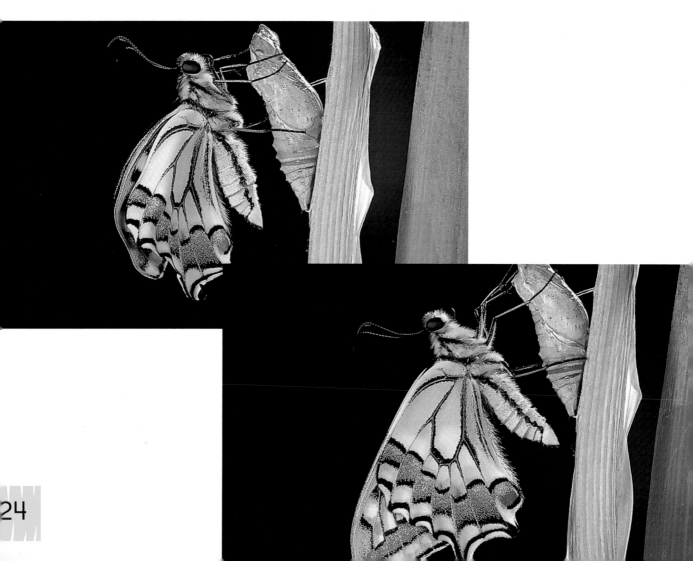

After 30 minutes, the wings have expanded to full size, but it will be a few hours before they can be used for flight.

Releasing your pets

If you have bred some butterflies or moths, release them in the place where you found the caterpillar foodplant. Do not release any species foreign to that area.

If you choose the right spot, you might start your own wild breeding colony.

Interesting facts

The largest moth is the Hercules Emperor Moth which can have a wingspan up to 300mm.

The migrating Monarch butterfly travels thousands of miles each year from Canada to spend winter in Mexico. It can also fly across the Atlantic Ocean to Britain.

Some Hawk Moths have tongues as long as 350mm to enable them to sip nectar from flowers while they are hovering above.

Butterfly and moth wings are covered in tiny dust-like scales. These make up the colourful patterns on their wings.

Silk cloth is made from the threads of the cocoon of a white silk moth such as the Bombyx mori.

Index